# HOW FRIENDS ARE PARTED

THERE WAS ONCE A RICH MERCHANT WHO WAS TRAVELLING ALONE THROUGH A FOREST IN A CART LOADED WITH GOODS FOR SALE.

IF ALL GOES WELL AND I SELL THESE GOODS, I WILL MAKE A LOT OF MONEY.

BUT ALL DID NOT GO WELL.

OH, NO!

IN THE SAME FOREST WERE TWO JACKALS, DAMANAKA AND KARATAKA, WHO WERE FAR FROM HAPPY.

WE HAVE FALLEN FROM KING LION'S FAVOUR. NO MORE FEASTS FOR US!

WE DON'T HAVE TO STARVE. WE CAN HUNT, CAN'T WE?

JUST THEN KING LION PASSED BY WITHOUT EVEN GLANCING AT THE TWO JACKALS.

KARATAKA, MARK MY WORDS. BY OUR EFFORTS WE WILL WIN BACK THE CONFIDENCE OF OUR KING.

THE LION APPROACHED A POOL OF WATER.

THAT WAS A GRAND FEAST. NOW FOR A LONG DEEP DRINK OF WATER, THEN ... SLEEP!

EVEN AS THE LION BEGAN TO DRINK ...

3

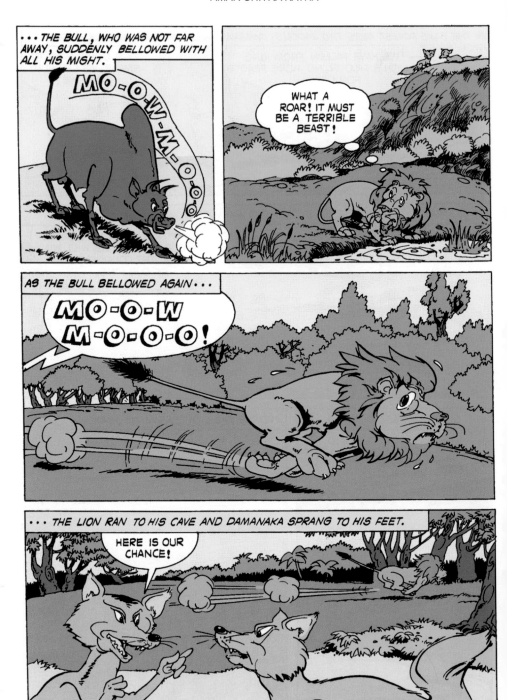

WHAT SHALL I DO?

MY BROTHER AND I CAN FIND A WAY TO HELP YOU.

WE WILL BE ALL THE MORE HELPFUL IF YOUR MAJESTY TREATS US TO A ROYAL FEAST.

IT SHALL BE DONE. SUMMON YOUR BROTHER AND ALL THE OTHER JACKALS.

THE JACKALS HOWLED FOR JOY WHEN THEY SAW THE MAGNIFICENT FEAST THAT LAY BEFORE THEM.

THIS IS A LAVISH SPREAD INDEED!

EAT, MY FRIEND. EAT AS MUCH AS YOU WISH!

WHEN THEY HAD FINISHED, DAMANAKA TOOK THE LION ASIDE.

MY BROTHER AND I ARE VERY GRATEFUL. WE WILL SOON SET YOUR FEARS AT REST.

I HOPE DAMANAKA KNOWS WHAT HE'S DOING.

DAMANAKA THEN WENT UP TO THE BULL.

O BULL, I AM THE KEEPER OF THIS FOREST. DON'T YOU KNOW YOU CAN'T COME HERE WITHOUT PERMISSION?

FRIEND, I COME FROM THE CITY. I DON'T KNOW THE WAYS OF THE FOREST. DO GUIDE ME.

DON'T ASK ME. ASK KARATAKA, THE KING'S GENERAL, WHO COMMANDS YOU TO APPEAR BEFORE HIM.

THE BULL WENT TO KARATAKA AND FELL AT HIS FEET.

O MIGHTY GENERAL, WHAT WOULD YOU HAVE ME DO?

YOU MUST GO AND FALL AT THE IMPERIAL FEET OF KING LION.

THE BULL WAS TERRIFIED.

WHAT IF HE ATTACKS ME?

FOOLISH BULL! MIGHTY CREATURES BATTLE ONLY WITH THE MIGHTY. HIS MAJESTY WILL NOT CONDESCEND TO FIGHT YOU. WE WILL TAKE YOU TO HIM.

AS THEY APPROACHED THE LION'S DEN —

YOU WAIT HERE. I WILL INFORM HIS MAJESTY THAT YOU ARE HERE TO PAY HIM HOMAGE.

THE LION GRACIOUSLY WELCOMED DAMANAKA. THEN —

HAVE YOU SEEN HIM?

I HAVE. HE IS AS DANGEROUS AS YOUR MAJESTY FEARED. BUT AFTER MUCH PERSUASION HE IS WILLING TO BE YOUR FRIEND.

WHERE IS HE?

HE IS HERE WAITING TO MEET YOU. PLEASE DON'T BE SO ALARMED.

YOUR MAJESTY, NOW THAT YOUR FEARS ARE SET AT REST, MAY I PROMISE MY BROTHER AND THE PACK ANOTHER FEAST?

NOT ONE FEAST, BUT MANY MORE. MY TREASURY OF FOOD IS OPEN TO YOUR PACK. I WILL NOW SEE THE ANIMAL.

DAMANAKA RETURNED TO HIS BROTHER AND THE TWO OF THEM LED THE BULL TO THE LION.

YOUR MAJESTY, I COME TO PAY YOU HOMAGE.

COME, COME, MY GOOD FRIEND! WE ARE EQUALS. ONLY A SUBORDINATE PAYS HOMAGE TO A SUPERIOR.

BE MY GUEST AND LIVE AS LONG AS YOU LIKE IN MY FOREST.

THE BULL WAS PLEASANTLY SURPRISED. HE CONTINUED LIVING IN THE FOREST, NOW AS THE HONOURED GUEST OF HIS MAJESTY, THE LION.

ONE DAY THE LION CAME UP TO THE BULL WITH ANOTHER LION.

FRIEND, PLEASE LOOK AFTER MY BROTHER WHILE I GO AND HUNT FOR SOME FOOD FOR HIM.

BUT, YOUR MAJESTY, WHAT ABOUT THE FLESH OF ALL THE ANIMALS THAT WERE SLAIN TODAY?

DAMANAKA THEN WENT IN SEARCH OF THE BULL.

AH! THERE HE IS! I MUST LOOK AS DEJECTED AS I CAN.

THE BULL CALLED OUT TO HIM.

WHY ARE YOU SO UNHAPPY?

THERE'S NOTHING BUT MISERY FOR THOSE WHO SERVE WICKED MASTERS.

AND DAMANAKA SIGHED.

WHAT DO YOU MEAN?

I SHOULD NOT BETRAY MY KING. BUT I HAD PROMISED YOU PROTECTION. HIS MAJESTY'S HEART IS TURNED AGAINST YOU.

WHAT MAKES YOU THINK THAT?

HE HAS MADE SECRET PLANS TO KILL YOU AND LET US FEAST ON YOUR FLESH.

15

THE BULL, MEANWHILE, HAD COME NEAR THE DEN.

THE JACKAL WAS RIGHT. HIS MAJESTY HAS CRUEL INTENTIONS. I WILL NOT DIE WITHOUT A FIGHT.

HE LOWERED HIS HORNS AND CHARGED.

THE LION SOON KILLED HIM. AS HE STOOD STARING AT THE CARCASS OF THE BULL, A WEIRD SOUND CAUGHT HIS EARS.

HE! HE! HE!
HE! HE! HE!

WHAT'S THAT I HEAR? THE GLEEFUL HOWL OF THE JACKALS! AH, I HAVE LET THE CUNNING JACKALS OUT-WIT ME AND PART ME FROM A TRUE FRIEND!

18

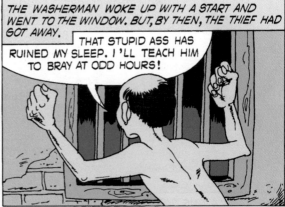

# THE CAT WHO SERVED A LION

ONCE UPON A TIME THERE LIVED A LION. HE WAS A MIGHTY BEAST BEFORE WHOM ALL TREMBLED...

...ALL EXCEPT A TINY MOUSE.

HA! HA! YOUR FINE MANE WILL MAKE A SOFT BED FOR MY LITTLE ONES WHEN THEY COME.

DAY AFTER DAY THE MOUSE NIBBLED AT THE LION'S MANE AS HE SLEPT IN HIS DEN.

EACH DAY WHEN THE LION WOKE UP —

AGAIN! MORE OF MY MAGNIFICENT MANE HAS GONE!

AH! THERE YOU ARE. WAIT TILL I CATCH YOU.

BUT THE LITTLE MOUSE QUICKLY SCUTTLED INTO HER HOLE.

SHE'S GONE! WELL, MICE ARE NOT MY PREY. I'M NO CAT.

21

23

BUT THE CAT HAD BEEN TOO HASTY.

I NO LONGER HEAR THE LITTLE PEST MOVE ABOUT. SHE MUST HAVE GONE SOMEWHERE ELSE.

AS THE DAYS PASSED, THE LION NO LONGER NEEDING THE CAT'S SERVICES, DID NOT BOTHER TO FEED HIM.

FRIEND LION, I'M HUNGRY.

THEN GO AND CATCH YOURSELF SOME MICE. I'D LIKE TO SLEEP NOW. DON'T DISTURB ME.

THE CAT LEFT THE DEN, A WISER ANIMAL.

I'VE BEEN A FOOL! I SHOULD NOT HAVE KILLED THAT MOUSE.

# THE TERRIBLE BELL

ONE AFTERNOON, WHEN ALL THE MEN OF BRAHMAPURA WERE AWAY AT WORK, A THIEF CAME TO THE VILLAGE TEMPLE.

OH! BAD LUCK! THE DOORS ARE CLOSED. THE ONLY THING I CAN TAKE AWAY IS THE BELL.

THE THIEF TOOK THE BELL···

···AND RAN TOWARDS THE HILLS.

I'LL CROSS THE HILLTOP AND SELL THIS IN ANOTHER VILLAGE. IT SHOULD FETCH A GOOD PRICE.

BUT THAT WAS NOT TO BE. FOR AS SOON AS HE ENTERED THE FOREST IN THE HILLS—

A TIGER! HELP! SAVE ME! E-E-AH!

THE TIGER KILLED HIM AND CARRIED HIM AWAY.

THE NEXT MORNING A TROOP OF MONKEYS CAME BY.

WHAT'S THIS?

I'VE SEEN ONE LIKE IT BEFORE. IT MAKES A FUNNY SOUND IF YOU SHAKE IT.

THE MONKEY SHOOK IT HARD.

TING! TING! CLANG! CLANG!

I BET I CAN MAKE A LOUDER SOUND!

CLANG

CLANG

JUST THEN —

CLANG, CLANG.

THERE! CAN YOU HEAR IT?

YES. IT MUST BE THE DEMON.

RUMOURS SPREAD ABOUT THE CRUEL DEMON.

HIS EARS RING LIKE BELLS AS HE SWINGS THEM ABOUT!

HE IS THE DEMON GHANTAKARNA!

HE IS A KILLER!

BUT ONE OF THE VILLAGERS, A WOMAN, WAS WISER.

I REFUSE TO BELIEVE THERE'S A DEMON THERE, UNLESS I SEE HIM WITH MY OWN EYES.

SHE THOUGHT DEEPLY FOR A WHILE. THEN —

THE NOISE SOUNDS LIKE THE CLANGING OF A BELL. I'M SURE SOME MONKEYS HAVE SOMEHOW GOT HOLD OF A BELL, AND····

MEANWHILE THE VILLAGERS WENT TO THEIR HEADMAN.

SIR, THERE IS A DEMON ON THE HILL.

WE ARE AFRAID HE'LL COME HERE AND KILL US.

WE WANT TO LEAVE THE VILLAGE.

AS THE HEADMAN WONDERED WHAT TO DO, THE WOMAN SPOKE UP.

SIR, PAY ME SOME MONEY AND I WILL CHASE THE DEMON AWAY.

THE HEADMAN COULD NOT BELIEVE HIS EARS.

YOU WILL CHASE HIM AWAY?

YES.

HE TURNED TO HIS ASSISTANT.

GIVE HER ALL THE MONEY SHE WANTS.

THE WOMAN TOOK THE MONEY AND WENT OUT—

I'LL NEED SOME MANGOES.

SO SHE BOUGHT SOME MANGOES...

...AND SET OUT FOR THE HILL.

IN THE FOREST SHE THREW THE MANGOES ABOUT...

IF MY GUESS IS RIGHT THE "DEMON" WILL COME OUT!

...AND HID BEHIND A TREE.

THE MONKEYS SMELT THE MANGOES AND CAME SCAMPERING UP.

MANGOES!

THE BELL WAS DROPPED IN THE DASH FOR THE MANGOES.

I WAS RIGHT! THERE'S NO DEMON HERE! ONLY SOME MONKEYS WITH A BELL!

COMING OUT FROM HER HIDING PLACE...

... SHE GRABBED THE BELL ...

... RAN BACK TO THE VILLAGE ...

... AND WENT TO THE HEADMAN.

HERE IS YOUR DEMON! THE TERRIBLE SOUND CAME FROM THIS HARM-LESS TEMPLE BELL.

IT WAS CLEVER OF YOU TO HAVE GUESSED THE TRUTH. YOU WILL BE REWARDED.

THE HEADMAN REWARDED HER AND FROM THAT DAY ON SHE BECAME THE MOST RESPECTED PERSON IN BRAHMAPURA.

# A BAG OF GOLD COINS

**The route to your roots**

# A BAG OF GOLD COINS

The precious bag contains the fruits of a lifetime of hard work. Thieves and scoundrels lay claim to it, but foolishness and downright dishonesty thwart their aspirations. As these tales reveal, fate eventually favours only the honest. The stories in this Amar Chitra Katha have been adapted from the *Anwar-i-Suhaili*, a Persian version of the Panchatantra, written by Hussain Ali Waiz in the 15th century. The tales were beautifully illustrated by famous artists in the court of Akbar and Jahangir.

**Script**
Shanti Devi Motichandra

**Illustrations**
V.B.Halbe

**Editor**
Anant Pal

# A BAG OF GOLD COINS

LONG, LONG AGO THERE LIVED A FARMER WHO ALWAYS WORKED HARD.

WITH HIS TOIL, HE RAISED A BUMPER CROP.

AT LAST MY LABOUR HAS BEEN REWARDED!

2

HE THEN OPENED THE DOOR. IT WAS A FRIEND OF HIS OUTSIDE.

I AM ON MY WAY TO THE MARKET. I THOUGHT YOU MIGHT LIKE TO JOIN ME.

I CERTAINLY WOULD!

AS HE WAS SETTING OUT, HE SAW HIS WIFE.

I'LL BE BACK BY NOON. KEEP LUNCH READY.

IN HIS HURRY HE FORGOT ALL ABOUT THE BAG OF COINS.

WHEN HIS WIFE ENTERED THE KITCHEN—

THERE ISN'T A DROP OF WATER IN THE HOUSE. I MUST FETCH SOME.

SHE TOOK A POT...

4

HE PUT DOWN THE POT AND EXAMINED THE BAG.

GOLD COINS, ALL OF THEM! THIS IS MY LUCKY DAY!

HE FORGOT ALL ABOUT THE WATER AND WALKED TOWARDS THE CITY.

I WILL GIVE A FEAST TO MY FRIENDS.

HE BOUGHT A FAT GOAT AT THE MARKET. ON HIS WAY BACK—

WHAT A FOOL AM I, TO CARRY THE BAG OPENLY!

I MUST HIDE IT IMMEDIATELY.

WHAT BETTER PLACE THAN THE GOAT'S INSIDE!

FATHER WILL BE PLEASED WITH THIS DEAL... IT'S BROUGHT HIM A PROFIT.

WHEN THE FARMER REACHED HOME—

WHAT A PLUMP GOAT!

YES. I INTEND TO GIVE A FEAST TO OUR FRIENDS. TIE IT UP IN THE BACKYARD.

AS THE FARMER ENTERED THE HOUSE—

MY POT! MY POT IS GONE!

WHERE IS THE POT WHICH I HAD KEPT HERE?

I GAVE IT TO THE BUTCHER TO FETCH WATER IN; HE HASN'T YET COME BACK.

WITHIN MINUTES, HE CAME RUSHING INTO THE KITCHEN.

YOU LOOK EXCITED. WHAT IS THE MATTER?

MY BAG OF COINS! MY TREASURE! I FOUND IT IN THE GOAT'S BELLY.

HOW DID IT GET IN THERE?

THE BUTCHER MUST HAVE STUFFED IT DOWN THE ANIMAL'S THROAT. I BOUGHT IT FROM HIS SON.

I'VE LEARNT MY LESSON. HENCEFORTH I'LL CARRY THE MONEY ON MY PERSON.

THE NEXT DAY, THE FARMER HAD TO GO TO TOWN ON BUSINESS. ON THE WAY BACK—

IT IS HOT. A DIP IN THE WATER WOULD BE PLEASANT.

LEAVING THE CLOTHES AND THE BAG OF COINS ON THE BANK, HE GOT INTO THE WATER.

A SHEPHERD WHO HAPPENED TO PASS THAT WAY SAW THE BAG.

GOLD COINS! THIS IS MY LUCKY DAY.

HE WALKED AWAY WITH THE BAG.

11

WHILE THE DEJECTED FARMER WAS WALKING HOMEWARDS, THERE CAME A STRONG WIND.

MY TURBAN!

CHASING THE TURBAN, THE FARMER REACHED THE WELL.

HELP!

MY TREASURE! I'VE FOUND IT!

HE CLIMBED OUT OF THE WELL...

...AND WENT HOME.

THE NEXT DAY, THE FARMER AND THE SHEPHERD RAN INTO EACH OTHER AT THE VILLAGE MARKET.

YOU LOOK UNHAPPY. WHAT'S THE MATTER?

I HAD HIDDEN A BAG OF GOLD COINS IN A WELL. NOW IT HAS DISAPPEARED.

THEN THE BAG I PICKED UP FROM THE WELL WAS NOT MINE.

YOUR MONEY IS SAFE. I FOUND THE BAG AND I THOUGHT IT WAS THE ONE I HAD LOST ON THE RIVER BANK. COME WITH ME AND I'LL GIVE IT TO YOU.

THE FARMER TOOK HIM HOME AND GAVE HIM THE BAG OF COINS.

I HOPE YOU SOON FIND YOUR BAG.

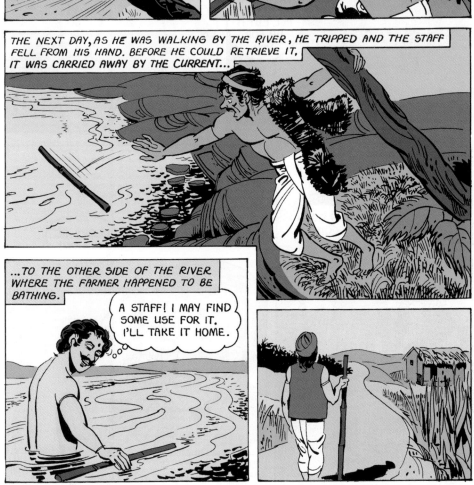

WHEN HE REACHED HOME—

THERE IS NO WOOD FOR FUEL.

WE CAN USE THIS STAFF I FOUND. I'LL CUT IT UP FOR YOU.

WHEN HE BROUGHT THE AXE DOWN ON THE STAFF—

MY GOLD COINS!

THRICE HAVE I LOST MY COINS AND THRICE HAVE I REGAINED THEM.

GLORY BE TO GOD!

**MORAL:** NOBODY CAN DEPRIVE US OF WHAT IS RIGHTFULLY OURS.

# THE UNGRATEFUL GOLDSMITH

ONCE UPON A TIME, A TRAVELLER WAS PASSING THROUGH A FOREST.

O GOOD MAN, HELP US OUT OF THIS WELL.

THE KIND-HEARTED TRAVELLER LOWERED A CREEPER INTO THE WELL...

...AND PULLED THE ANIMALS UP.

I CAN'T LEAVE HIM TO DIE OF STARVATION. I WILL HELP HIM OUT.

WE WISH YOU WOULD HEED OUR ADVICE.

SOON THE MAN TOO WAS OUT OF THE WELL.

I AM A GOLDSMITH. YOU MUST VISIT ME AT MY HOUSE IN THE CITY.

A YEAR LATER, THE TRAVELLER RETURNED TO THE SAME SPOT WITH A BAG OF GOLD COINS.

IT IS GETTING DARK. LET ME REST NOW. TOMORROW I SHALL SEEK MY FRIENDS.

AS HE SLEPT, A BAND OF ROBBERS HAPPENED TO PASS BY.

THEY TIED HIM UP...

...PUSHED HIM DOWN THE EDGE OF A PRECIPICE...

...AND RAN AWAY WITH HIS BAG OF GOLD COINS.

AT THAT MOMENT, THE MONKEY WHO HAPPENED TO BE NEAR BY, HEARD SOMEONE CRYING FOR HELP.

THAT VOICE SOUNDS FAMILIAR. LET ME SEE WHO IT IS.

HELP! HELP!

AH! IT'S YOU! DO NOT WORRY, MY FRIEND. I'LL SET YOU FREE IN NO TIME.

FORTUNATELY FOR THE TRAVELLER, HE HAD FALLEN ON A HEAP OF GRASS.

THE MONKEY RESCUED HIM.

AS HE RESTED UNDER A TREE, THE TRAVELLER TOLD HIS TALE.

YOU STAY HERE AND RELAX. I'LL BRING YOU YOUR BAG OF GOLD COINS.

IT DID NOT TAKE THE MONKEY LONG TO FIND THE ROBBERS.

GOOD! THEY ARE ALL ASLEEP.

HE TOOK THEIR POSSESSIONS AND HID THEM IN A BUSH NEAR BY.

WHEN THE ROBBERS WOKE UP—

HEY! OUR SWORDS! OUR BOXES! WHERE ARE THEY?

SOME EVIL SPIRIT HAS WHISKED THEM AWAY.

THE JUBILANT MONKEY CARRIED THE BAG OF COINS TO THE TRAVELLER.

HERE IS YOUR BAG OF COINS.

YOU HAVE BEEN KIND TO ME, MY FRIEND.

THE TRAVELLER TOOK THE BAG OF COINS AND WENT ON HIS WAY. BUT SOON—

GRRR...

OH, GOD! A LION!

DON'T BE AFRAID. I AM YOUR FRIEND. DON'T YOU REMEMBER ME?

WHY, YOU ARE THE LION OF THE WELL!

YOU ARE RIGHT. COME TO MY CAVE AND BE MY GUEST.

AT THE CAVE—

I HAVE A PRESENT FOR YOU. PLEASE ACCEPT IT.

YOU ARE VERY GENEROUS, O KING OF BEASTS.

AS THE TRAVELLER SET OUT FOR THE CITY—

HOW GRATEFUL THE ANIMALS HAVE BEEN! NOW LET ME VISIT THE GOLDSMITH.

WHEN HE REACHED THE CITY, THE NEXT MORNING —

OUR PRINCESS IS KILLED!

DO YOU KNOW WHO DID IT?

IT IS HARD TO FIND SOMEONE IN THIS EXCITED CROWD WHO WILL GUIDE ME TO THE GOLDSMITH.

FORTUNATELY THE GOLDSMITH ALSO HAPPENED TO BE IN THAT CROWD.

MY FRIEND, IT IS A PLEASURE TO MEET YOU AGAIN. PLEASE COME HOME WITH ME.

I AM GLAD THAT YOU REMEMBER ME.

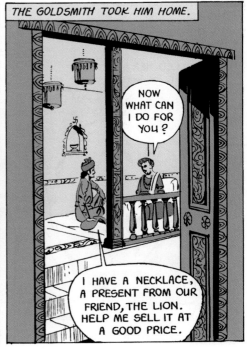

THE GOLDSMITH TOOK HIM HOME.

NOW WHAT CAN I DO FOR YOU?

I HAVE A NECKLACE, A PRESENT FROM OUR FRIEND, THE LION. HELP ME SELL IT AT A GOOD PRICE.

WHILE TAKING OUT THE NECKLACE FROM THE BAG, THE TRAVELLER SPILLED A FEW COINS.

I WISH I COULD GET MY HAND ON THOSE GOLD COINS.

LET ME HELP YOU.

THE GOLDSMITH GATHERED THE COINS AND HANDED THEM BACK TO THE TRAVELLER.

HERE IS THE NECKLACE. AND I ALSO ENTRUST THIS BAG OF GOLD COINS TO YOU. RETURN IT TO ME WHEN I LEAVE.

YOU CAN TRUST ME WITH YOUR BAG OF GOLD COINS. AND I SHALL SELL YOUR NECKLACE FOR A HIGH PRICE.

THIS LOOKS LIKE THE NECKLACE OF THE PRINCESS. THE LION MUST HAVE KILLED HER AND GOT IT.

I WILL INFORM THE KING ABOUT THE NECKLACE. THE TRAVELLER WILL BE SUSPECTED AND HANGED. I WILL BE REWARDED AND THE COINS WILL BE MINE FOREVER.

27

NO ONE WILL BE ABLE TO CURE HER OF MY POISON. THEN YOU GO TO THE PALACE...

...AND SAVE HER WITH THIS HERB. THE KING IS BOUND TO REWARD YOU.

GIVING HIM THE HERB, THE SNAKE WENT AWAY.

AFTER A WHILE, AT THE PALACE—

I'VE BEEN BITTEN BY A SNAKE! SAVE ME!

THE LEARNED MEN OF MEDICINE ALL CAME THERE.

WE HAVE TRIED ALL THE REMEDIES KNOWN TO US BUT IN VAIN, YOUR MAJESTY.

AS THE TRAVELLER CONCLUDED HIS STORY—

THE PRINCESS MIGHT HAVE BEEN KILLED BY THE LION. THE GREEDY GOLDSMITH LIED ABOUT ME.

HE SHALL BE PUNISHED. NOW PLEASE CURE HER.

THE TRAVELLER MIXED THE HERB IN A GLASS OF MILK...

...AND MADE THE QUEEN MOTHER DRINK IT.

MOTHER! DO YOU FEEL BETTER?

I DO, MY SON. SEE THAT THE ONE WHO SAVED MY LIFE IS AMPLY REWARDED.

THE KING TURNED TO THE TRAVELLER.

PLEASE ACCEPT THIS BAG OF GOLD COINS.

THANK YOU, YOUR MAJESTY.

BY THEN IT WAS DAYBREAK. THE GOLDSMITH WAS WAITING AT THE PLACE OF EXECUTION.

THE TRAVELLER HAS NOT YET BEEN BROUGHT. ONCE HE IS HANGED, I'M SAFE.

JUST THEN THE KING'S SOLDIERS CAME THERE AND SEIZED HIM.

YOU ARE THE GUILTY ONE! YOU ARE TO BE HANGED! THE KING'S ORDERS.

**MORAL:** EVIL IS ALWAYS REWARDED WITH EVIL.

# CHOICE OF FRIENDS

**The route to your roots**

# CHOICE OF FRIENDS

Narayana, the author of these parables, insists that we exercise caution when choosing our companions. His charming animal characters – sometimes silly, sometimes wise – remind us of ourselves. We learn to avoid the pitfalls of life, along with his animal characters, thus attaining wisdom in a rather enjoyable way! Most importantly, we realise the worth of an honest friend.

**Script**
Kamala Chandakant

**Illustrations**
Jeffrey Fowler

**Editor**
Anant Pai

# CHOICE OF FRIENDS

ONE DAY AT THE BREAK OF DAWN, A CROW PERCHED ON A TREE NEAR THE RIVER GODAVARI, SAW A FOWLER APPROACHING.

O LORD! HERE COMES YAMA* IN PERSON. I WONDER WHAT HE IS UP TO.

THE FOWLER FIXED HIS NET...

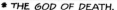

* THE GOD OF DEATH.

1

... SCATTERED SOME RICE ON THE GROUND ...

... AND HID HIMSELF IN THE HOLLOW OF A TREE.

A LITTLE LATER, THE KING OF THE PIGEONS AND HIS FLOCK HAPPENED TO FLY PAST.

LOOK! DO YOU SEE THOSE GRAINS?

O KING, LET US FEAST ON THEM.

NO! I SUSPECT A TRAP. HOW DID THOSE GRAINS COME HERE?

HE IS WISE.

BEWARE! GREED CAN LEAD US TO DOOM AS IT DID THE GREEDY TRAVELLER.

AND HE TOLD THEM THE STORY OF THE TIGER AND THE TRAVELLER. AT THE END OF THE STORY THE MAJORITY OF THE PIGEONS AGREED WITH HIM, WHEN —

O BROTHERS, MUST WE GIVE UP A FEAST FOR VAGUE FEARS?

FOOL! FOOL!

CHOICE OF FRIENDS

3

HE PONDERED FOR A WHILE. THEN—

YES! WE WILL FLY OFF WITH THE NET.

GET READY! WHEN I GIVE THE SIGNAL, ALL OF YOU TAKE OFF AT THE SAME TIME.

AT THAT MOMENT THE FOWLER, DELIGHTED WITH HIS CATCH, CAME OUT OF HIDING.

QUICK! ONE! TWO! THREE! UP!

BRAVO! I'LL FOLLOW THEM AND SEE WHAT THEY DO NEXT.

FLAP FLAP

FLAP

THE FOWLER RAN FORWARD WAVING HIS ARMS.

HEY! STOP! MY NET!

BUT ALL HIS WAVING WAS OF NO USE.

THERE GOES MY NET. I MAY AS WELL RETURN HOME.

HOW SHALL WE GET RID OF THIS WRETCHED NET, O KING?

I TOO, WONDER!

A FRIEND OF MINE, THE KING OF THE MICE, LIVES IN THE FOREST NEAR BY. WE WILL GO TO HIM. HE WILL CUT OUR BONDS.

DOWN IN HIS RETREAT WHEN THE MOUSE HEARD THE COMMOTION CAUSED BY THE DESCENDING PIGEONS, HE WAS ALARMED.

STRANGE SOUNDS! IT MAY BE SOME UNKNOWN DANGER AGAINST WHICH I MIGHT BE HELPLESS. I'D BE SAFER INSIDE.

FLAP FLAP

WHEN THE PIGEON COULD NOT SEE HIS FRIEND —

FRIEND MOUSE, AREN'T YOU GOING TO WELCOME US?

WHY IT'S MY GOOD OLD FRIEND!

A. MOUSE

THE MOUSE RUSHED OUT.

I AM DELIGHTED TO SEE YOU...

A. MOUSE

...BUT WHAT IS THIS? YOU SEEM TO BE TRAPPED IN A NET!

HE RAN FORWARD AND WAS ABOUT TO GNAW AT THE STRINGS WHEN —

NO, MY FRIEND. FIRST FREE MY FOLLOWERS.

BUT I AM SMALL AND MY TEETH TINY. SUPPOSE MY STRENGTH FAILS ME BEFORE I FREE YOU.

IT DOES NOT MATTER. MY DUTY IS TO PROTECT MY SUBJECTS, AT THE COST OF MY LIFE IF NEED BE.

NO! NO! I WILL FIRST FREE YOU. AND THEN ATTEND TO THE OTHERS. IT IS NOT WISE TO SACRIFICE ONESELF TO PRESERVE ONE'S DEPENDANTS.

THAT MAY BE TRUE. BUT DEATH WHICH COMES TO ALL COMES NOBLY WHEN WE GIVE OUR LIFE, OUR ALL, TO SAVE ANOTHER'S LIFE. YOU WILL FREE THEM FIRST.

SUCH NOBILITY IS RARE.

THE MOUSE WAS MOVED.

NOBLY SPOKEN, FRIEND PIGEON, NOBLY SPOKEN. I SHALL DO AS YOU WISH.

I KNEW YOU WOULD.

THE MOUSE BEGAN FREEING THE PIGEONS.

POOR, BRAVE, MOUSE. CAN HE HOLD OUT?

6

THE MOUSE DID HOLD OUT. HIS FRIEND'S NOBILITY GAVE HIM THE STRENGTH.

AS SOON AS YOU ARE FREE, YOU MUST LET ME TREAT YOU AND YOUR FOLLOWERS TO A FEAST.

A TRUE FRIEND INDEED. I WILL MAKE HIM MY FRIEND TOO.

THEN, THANKING THE MOUSE, THE PIGEON AND HIS FOLLOWERS FLEW AWAY.

AS THE MOUSE WAS ABOUT TO GO BACK TO HIS RETREAT, THE CROW FLEW DOWN TO HIM.

O STAUNCH FRIEND, LET ME TOO BE YOUR FRIEND.

THE MOUSE WAS AMUSED.

HOW CAN THAT BE? I AM YOUR NATURAL FOOD. THE NEXT THING I KNOW, YOU WILL BE EATING ME. WE CAN NEVER BE FRIENDS.

AND THE MOUSE TOLD HIM THE STORY OF THE DEER, THE JACKAL AND THE CROW.*

BUT AT THE END OF IT —

YOU NEED HAVE NO FEAR OF THAT. YOU ARE TOO TINY TO BE EVEN A FULL BREAKFAST FOR ME.

9

SO THE TWO FRIENDS SET OFF FOR THE FOREST WHERE THE TORTOISE LIVED.

WHEN THE TORTOISE SAW THE CROW, HE WAS OVERJOYED.

WHAT BRINGS YOU HERE, MY GOOD OLD FRIEND?

FOOD WAS SCARCE IN OUR FOREST.

AND WHOM HAVE YOU BROUGHT ALONG?

MY LOYAL FRIEND, THE KING OF THE MICE. HE IS THE MOST VIRTUOUS AND KIND SOUL I'VE EVER MET.

WELCOME TO OUR FOREST, O MOUSE. THERE IS ENOUGH FOOD HERE FOR ALL OF US, AND MORE.

AND SO THE THREE FRIENDS LIVED HAPPILY TOGETHER. ONE DAY, AS THE TORTOISE WAS ABOUT TO GO FOR A SWIM IN THE TANK, A DEER CAME PANTING UP TO THEM.

WHAT'S THE MATTER?

A HUNTER. HE'S AFTER ME.

COME FRIEND, REFRESH YOURSELF WITH SOME GRASS AND WATER. MY FRIENDS WILL LOOK AFTER YOU. I AM GOING FOR A SWIM AND SHALL JOIN YOU LATER.

THE DEER HAD HIS REPAST AS THEY WAITED FOR THE TORTOISE.

WE MUST FLEE FROM HERE. I TOOK A SHORT CUT. THE HUNTER WILL SOON DISCOVER THIS FOREST. IT'S ON HIS ROUTE.

THEN WE MUST LEAVE THIS FOREST.

YES, IT WOULD BE SAFER.

BUT HOW WILL GOOD OLD TORTOISE MAKE IT ACROSS THE LAND?

SUDDENLY—

HELP! HELP!

ALAS! OUR FRIEND HAS BEEN CAUGHT!

THE HUNTER PICKED UP THE TORTOISE AND FIXED HIM ON HIS BOW.

DON'T DESPAIR! QUICK. WE STILL HAVE A CHANCE TO RESCUE HIM.

DEER, GO AND LIE ACROSS THE HUNTER'S PATH, AS IF DEAD. QUICK!

FRIEND CROW WILL HOVER OVER YOU AND PECK AT YOUR BODY.

WHEN HE SEES YOU, HE WILL PUT FRIEND TORTOISE DOWN. AND I WILL GNAW AT THE BINDING STRINGS.

THE DEER AND THE CROW TOOK THEIR POSITIONS. AS EXPECTED, THE HUNTER SOON CAME BY.

A DEER! IT'S BEEN A GOOD DAY FOR ME.

HE PUT THE TORTOISE DOWN AND DREW HIS KNIFE.

SHOO! SHOO!

MEANWHILE —

THERE! YOU'RE FREE. QUICK! INTO THE WATER.

I MUST BE ALERT... SPRING UP... AND RUN.

WELL, NEVER MIND. I STILL HAVE MY TORTOISE.

BUT WHEN HE GOT BACK TO THE SPOT WHERE HE HAD LEFT THE TORTOISE —

ALAS! THE FELLOW HAS ESCAPED. I DESERVE IT FOR BEING SO GREEDY.

THAT WAS A NEAT PLAN, FRIEND MOUSE. YOU SAVED MY LIFE.

DON'T SINGLE ME OUT. EACH OF YOUR FRIENDS RISKED HIS LIFE TO SAVE YOURS — LIKE MY FRIEND, THE KING OF THE PIGEONS.

13

# THE TIGER AND THE TRAVELLER

ONE DAY A TIGER, TOO OLD TO HUNT, WAS WALKING BY A MARSHY POOL WHEN HE SAW A GOLD BANGLE.

I MAY AS WELL PICK IT UP. IT COULD BE OF SOME USE.

I'VE GOT THE BAIT. NOW I MUST WAIT FOR THE CATCH.

JUST THEN A TRAVELLER PASSED BY THE OPPOSITE BANK.

HE LOOKED AT THE TIGER.

HM-M-M. I'D LOVE TO HAVE THE BANGLE. BUT HOW CAN I TRUST A FIERCE BEAST LIKE YOU?

YOU HAVE EVERY REASON TO SUSPECT ME. I HAVE BEEN WICKED IN MY TIME. BUT NOW? ON THE ADVICE OF A SANYASI I AM CHANGED. SO COME ACROSS AND TAKE THIS.

IF I COME CLOSE, YOU MAY FORGET THE SANYASI'S ADVICE WHEN YOU SMELL ME.

I WON'T. BESIDES I'M OLD. MY CLAWS ARE BLUNT. SO DO NOT FEAR. COME, WADE ACROSS THE POOL AND TAKE THIS.

THE TRAVELLER'S LOVE OF GOLD OVERCAME HIS NATURAL FEAR OF THE TIGER.

HE SEEMS TO BE TELLING THE TRUTH.

I WILL WADE ACROSS AND TAKE IT.

BUT HARDLY HAD HE TAKEN A FEW STEPS WHEN –

OH! OH! IT'S A MIRE! I'M STUCK! HELP!

THE TIGER WADED MENACINGLY UP TO THE TRAVELLER...

... AND POUNCED ON HIM.

# THE CROW, THE DEER AND THE JACKAL

LONG, LONG AGO THERE LIVED A DEER AND A CROW. THEY WERE GOOD FRIENDS AND LOVED EACH OTHER DEARLY.

ONE DAY A JACKAL SAW THE DEER.

WHAT A DELICIOUS MEAL HE WOULD MAKE. MM-M-M!

HE WENT UP TO THE DEER.

GOOD DAY, MY FRIEND.

WHO ARE YOU?

19

I AM A LONELY JACKAL. I HAVE NO FRIENDS. BUT NOW THAT I HAVE MET YOU, I HAVE ONE. WILL YOU BE MY FRIEND?

THE DEER WAS MOVED BY HIS WORDS.

POOR JACKAL. OF COURSE I'LL BE YOUR FRIEND. COME, LET ME TAKE YOU TO MY FRIEND, CROW.

WHEN THE CROW SAW THE TWO TOGETHER, HE WAS SURPRISED.

WHO'S THIS?

MY FRIEND, JACKAL. HE IS LONELY AND SEEKS OUR FRIENDSHIP.

DON'T YOU KNOW THAT YOU MUST THINK TWICE BEFORE MAKING UTTER STRANGERS YOUR FRIENDS?

NO! BUT WHY?

THE CROW TOLD HIM THE STORY OF THE VULTURE, THE CAT AND THE BIRDS. *AT THE END OF IT—

...AND THAT IS WHY ONE SHOULD ALWAYS BE WARY OF STRANGERS.

BUT THE JACKAL WAS NOT TO BE TALKED OUT OF HIS DINNER BY SUCH ADVICE.

SIR CROW, YOU SEEM TO FORGET THAT ON THE FIRST DAY HE MET YOU, YOU TOO WERE A STRANGER TO HIM. AND YET YOUR FRIENDSHIP ONLY GROWS STRONGER EACH DAY.

HE IS MY FRIEND. WHY DON'T YOU ALSO BE MY FRIEND?

THE DEER DID NOT LIKE SCENES.

COME, FRIEND CROW, LET US ALL LIVE TOGETHER IN AMITY AND JOY.

ALL RIGHT. DO AS YOU WISH.

SO THEY BEGAN LIVING TOGETHER. IN THE MORNING EACH WENT IN SEARCH OF HIS OWN FOOD AND...

... RETURNED LATE AT NIGHT.

ONE MORNING A FEW DAYS LATER, WHEN THE CROW HAD LEFT—

FRIEND DEER, IN ONE CORNER OF THIS FOREST THERE IS A FIELD FULL OF SWEET GRAIN. LET ME SHOW IT TO YOU. COME.

THE INNOCENT DEER ACCOMPANIED HIM AND GRAZED IN THE FIELD.

THIS GRAIN IS INDEED VERY SWEET. I SHALL COME HERE EVERY DAY AND FEED ON IT.

HA! HA! AND I WILL SOON FEED ON YOU.

ONE DAY, AS THE JACKAL HAD HOPED, THE OWNER OF THE FIELD SAW THE DEER.

AHA! SO YOU ARE THE THIEF WHO EATS MY CROPS. HM-M-M!

HE SET A SNARE TO CATCH THE DEER.

OH! OH! HELP! I'M TRAPPED. THIS IS THE END OF ME IF MY FRIENDS DON'T COME AND RESCUE ME.

THE JACKAL, WHO WAS WAITING AND WATCHING, CHUCKLED TO HIMSELF.

HO! HO! MY PATIENCE HAS BORNE FRUIT. WHEN THE FARMER CUTS HIM UP HIS BONES AND GRISTLE AND BLOOD WILL GIVE ME SOME DELICIOUS DINNERS!

THE DEER CAUGHT SIGHT OF HIM AND HEAVED A SIGH OF RELIEF.

QUICK! DEAR FRIEND, YOU ARE JUST IN TIME. GNAW AT THIS NET AND FREE ME.

TO HIS DISMAY THE JACKAL REFUSED.

I'M SORRY, MY FRIEND. THIS NET IS MADE OF SINEWS. SINCE I AM FASTING TODAY, I CANNOT BITE THEM. IT WOULD BE A SIN. I'LL COME AND FREE YOU TOMORROW, TO BE SURE.

AND HE WENT AWAY

23

WHEN THE CROW RETURNED HOME THAT EVENING AND DID NOT SEE HIS FRIEND, HE WAS WORRIED.

WHERE COULD HE BE? I HOPE HE IS NOT IN DANGER. I STILL DON'T TRUST THAT JACKAL.

AFTER SEARCHING EVERYWHERE FOR HIS FRIEND, HE CAME UPON THE FIELD.

ALAS! MY POOR DEAR FRIEND. HOW DID THIS HAPPEN?

THE JACKAL ...I SHOULD HAVE TAKEN YOUR ADVICE.

AH! THE TRAITOR! THE SLY KNAVE! WELL, I WARNED YOU.

I KNOW!

NEVER MIND. WHERE IS THAT RASCAL?

HE IS WAITING SOMEWHERE NEAR BY. WAITING TO TASTE MY FLESH. FLY AWAY LEST YOU TOO FALL INTO DANGER.

NO! DEAR FRIEND, I SHALL WAIT WITH YOU TILL THE END. PERHAPS I MIGHT STILL SAVE YOU.

THE CROW RACKED HIS BRAINS BUT COULD FIND NO WAY OUT. AT LAST DAY BROKE.

ALAS! THERE COMES THE FARMER WITH HIS CLUB. IF ONLY I COULD THINK OF SOME MEANS TO SAVE MY FRIEND.

SUDDENLY AN IDEA STRUCK HIM.

I HAVE IT! LIE ON YOUR BACK, PUFF YOUR STOMACH OUT, STIFFEN YOUR LEGS AND BE VERY STILL. I WILL PECK AT YOUR EYES. THEN WHEN I CROAK, SPRING TO YOUR FEET AND RUN FOR YOUR LIFE.

THE DEER DID EXACTLY AS HE WAS TOLD. WHEN THE FARMER CAME UP TO HIM —

AHA! THE FELLOW IS DEAD — OF FRIGHT NO DOUBT. WELL, THAT MAKES MY TASK EASIER.

HE BEGAN REMOVING THE NET.

25

AS HE WAS BUSY FOLDING IT —

THE DEER SPRANG UP AND MADE OFF.

ANNOYED AT HAVING BEEN TRICKED, HE FLUNG HIS CLUB.

IT HIT THE JACKAL AND KILLED HIM ON THE SPOT.

THE END

# THE VULTURE, THE CAT AND THE BIRDS

ONE DAY A BLIND OLD VULTURE CAME TO LIVE IN THE HOLLOW OF A TREE, WHERE BIRDS ROOSTED AT NIGHT.

THE BIRDS HELD A HURRIED CONFERENCE.

POOR OLD BIRD. HE CAN HARDLY MOVE AROUND. LET US GIVE HIM A SHARE OF OUR FOOD OR ELSE HE WILL SOON DIE OF STARVATION.

THE OLD VULTURE WAS TOUCHED BY THEIR KINDNESS.

I SHALL MAKE IT MY DUTY TO PROTECT THEIR YOUNG WHEN THEY ARE AWAY GATHERING FOOD.

ONE DAY A CAT HAPPENED TO PASS BY, WHEN THE BIRDS WERE AWAY. HE DID NOT SEE THE VULTURE WHO WAS NAPPING, PERCHED ON A HIGH BRANCH.

AHA! NESTS AND NESTS OF LITTLE FLEDGLINGS. FOOD ENOUGH FOR DAYS AND DAYS.

WHEN THE LITTLE BIRDS SAW THE CAT APPROACH, THEY SET UP SUCH A TWITTER THAT THE VULTURE WOKE UP.

HE SWOOPED DOWN.

WHO GOES THERE?

A VULTURE! OH! OH! I'M DONE FOR!

JUST THEN HE NOTICED SOMETHING.

OHO! THE FELLOW'S BLIND, AND HIS TALONS BLUNT WITH AGE. WHAT A RELIEF.

WHO GOES THERE, SPEAK UP!

I AM A CAT.

BE OFF! OR I'LL SLAY YOU.

I AM PREPARED TO DIE IF I DESERVE IT. BUT MAY I FIRST EXPLAIN WHY I AM HERE.

YES! YOU MAY.

I LIVE ON THE BANKS OF THE GANGA. THE BIRDS THERE CONSTANTLY SPEAK OF YOUR WISDOM AND YOUR LEARNING. I HAVE COME TO STUDY LAW FROM YOU.

YES. BUT CATS LIKE MEAT AND THERE ARE YOUNG BIRDS HERE. I WILL HAVE TO SLAY YOU.

O WISE BIRD, WOULD YOU KILL A STRANGER WHO COMES TO YOU AS A DISCIPLE? BESIDES, I KNOW THE SCRIPTURES AND I'VE OVERCOME PASSION.

HE SEEMS TO BE TRUSTWORTHY.

ALL RIGHT. YOU MAY LIVE IN THE HOLLOW WITH ME.

DAY AFTER DAY, THE CAT STOLE SOME FLEDGLINGS AND...

TIP TOE TIP

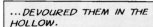

...DEVOURED THEM IN THE HOLLOW.

EACH EVENING WHEN THE BIRDS RETURNED HOME, THEY FOUND SOME FLEDGLINGS MISSING.

WE MUST INVESTIGATE THE MATTER.

IT'S TIME TO MOVE TO FRESH HUNTING GROUNDS.

HE SLUNK AWAY AS SOON AS POSSIBLE.

MEANWHILE AS THE BIRDS FLEW HITHER AND THITHER, ONE OF THEM CHIRRUPED LOUDLY.

TWEET! TWEET! SEE WHAT I'VE FOUND. I'VE GOT THE CULPRIT!

THE UNGRATEFUL WRETCH. HE HAS REPAID OUR KINDNESS BY EATING OUR HELPLESS ONES.

HE MUST BE PECKED TO DEATH.

SO THEY PECKED TO DEATH THE POOR VULTURE WHOSE ONLY FAULT WAS THAT HE TREATED AS A FRIEND ONE WITH WHOM HE WAS BARELY ACQUAINTED.

The End.